Alms for Oblivion

poems by

Robert E. Wood

Finishing Line Press
Georgetown, Kentucky

Alms for Oblivion

Copyright © 2017 by Robert E. Wood
ISBN 978-1-63534-153-9 First Edition
All rights reserved under International and Pan-American Copyright Conventions.
No part of this book may be reproduced in any manner whatsoever without written permission from the publisher, except in the case of brief quotations embodied in critical articles and reviews.

ACKNOWLEDGMENTS

Blue Fifth Review: Hyde on Jekyll
Calamaro: Spaghetti Western Hero
Eye Socket Journal: Everything Happens to Me
flashquake: In Defense of Catherine Deneuve
Flutter Poetry Journal: The Forest Fire
North Dakota Quarterly: Cold War
Rose and Thorn Journal: Weary Willie, Tuba Player, Shark Week, New Yorker Cartoon Dog, Bouquet of Daffodils for Daffy Duck, Viola
Sliver of Stone Magazine: Backlot
StepAway Magazine: Oxford in July
Stoney Lonesome: The Count to His Lover

Many thanks to family, friends and colleagues, to Colin Potts and the NDYP (JC Reilly, Blake Leland, and Karen Head), to Poetry at Tech and Poetry Atlanta, and to my editors.

Publisher: Leah Maines

Editor: Christen Kincaid

Cover Art: The Forest Fire, Piero di Cosimo, Public Domain

Author Photo: Colin Potts

Cover Design: Elizabeth Maines

Printed in the USA on acid-free paper.
Order online: www.finishinglinepress.com
       also available on amazon.com

Author inquiries and mail orders:
Finishing Line Press
P. O. Box 1626
Georgetown, Kentucky 40324
U. S. A.

Table of Contents

RETURN TO WORCESTER

Return to Worcester 1
Oxford in July 2
Ashmolean 3
    The Forest Fire
    Nature Morte
    Morris Dance
Turner in Venice 6
Thomas Coryate 7
Twilight 8
Ennui 9
Blenheim Jottings 10
On Following a Sign 11
American Poets Abroad 12
Viola 13

MONKEY MUSIC

Weary Willie 16
Everything Happens to Me 17
New Yorker Cartoon Dog 18
Bouquet of Daffodils for Daffy Duck 19
Shark Week 20
Spaghetti Western Hero 21
Tuba Player 22
Backlot 23
Dodge 24
The Count to His Lover 25
To the Queen 26
Hyde on Jekyll 27
Cold War 28
In Defense of Catherine Deneuve 29
Paperback Lady Private Eye 30

For Carolyn

Return to Worcester

Return to Worcester

By the martext heraldry
of omniscient porters

the Aylesbury ducks
magical as stolen foxgloves

become the martlets
of the Worcester crest.

The fox knows better,
their numbers have diminished.

Oxford in July

Walk out early to watch the city of Oxford
wake by the clock.
Perhaps the Friends are gathered somewhere quietly,
but no one hurries to a shrine or shop.

After a while, a cautious rectitude
begins behind the counters; buses arrive,
the vague meandering commences in the streets;
mendicant murmurs arise from doorways.

In gardens locked behind the college gates
larkspur pyramids flare violet in the heat.
The dreaming spires dream of Michaelmas.

Ashmolean

The Forest Fire
Piero di Cosimo

The human faces on a pig and deer,
perhaps a whim, suggest enigma.

The fire itself is almost afterthought.
Soon no creature will take notice.

Starling and peregrine are on display,
a Leonardo lesson in their flight.

Lion and lioness seem innocent,
almost a bestiary exercise.

An ox stands prominent, tawny and well-fleshed.
In the distance or some time later,

depending on convention, a herdsman
brandishing a yoke trails after oxen.

And for Piero, this yoke may mark the end
of the imagined, peaceable kingdom,

the beginning of friars chanting,
children crying, men coughing in the night.

Nature Morte

A small room chills
lest lobsters spoil
or fish shining
like silver goblets
distinguish themselves.

In a warmer chamber
Constable's precision
shadows clouds.
No window opens
to the sky.

Morris Dance
Dante Gabriel Rossetti: Proserpine

Janey inclines
to reverie.
Playing Proserpine
becomes her.

Waves of her hair
embrace the dark.
Her lips have touched
a mortal skin.

The pomegranate
bitten
bares its flesh.
Seeds are promises.

Turner in Venice

We are informed
that Ruskin's frigid charity
consumed intemperate sketches
of courtesans at rest.

Mumbles and Oystermouth
are spared the word
that Turner's Venice
wasn't simply stone.

The soft moan of pigeons
can deceive the ear.
The splash of water
whispers to the flesh.

Thomas Coryate
Mid-Sommer in Venice

Never
eye, ear, tongue
saw, heard, spoke
shape, song, praise
of such lubricious ladies
on those summer days.

For all we can surmise
he may have left as innocent as he arrived.

Twilight
Walter Sickert: The Brighton Pierrots

As if from the wing stage right
we view the Pierrots
although the scene takes place
at Brighton by the sea.

One of the company kicks up his heels
behind a pillar that obscures our sight
as does the darkness now fresh fallen.
The soubrette watches from across the stage.

The canvas seems a little brighter
as we back away--straw hats,
lamplight, the last red tint at the horizon.
Beneath the sadness of the Pierrots, a solace.

Ennui
Walter Richard Sickert 1913

If they were listening to music
we might feel differently
about this man and woman
we presume are man and wife.

She gazes at a bell jar full of birds.
The woman in the painting on the wall
would hint at a desire unextinguished
if there were music.

What then is sinister about a good cigar,
an air of contemplation,
a glass that looms too large,
silence and unlikely shadow?

Blenheim Jottings

Too many water spaniel wigs
watch from the high walls.
The more salacious histories
have been disneyfied; doors open
at a recorded prompt.

The ghosts have exited as we must
through the gift shop
and Blenheim stands cashiered
by a randy Queen, whose peccadillos
now would grace the tabloids on a rainy day

at Wimbledon. Still there is Churchill
undiminished, Blenheim's finest hour,
and the landscape turned a chilly Turner
delights the poet's eye, threatens the throat.
The sky is always *terra incognita* and unmapped.

On Following a Sign: Historic Church & Public Toilets
St. Mary's in Bibury

Stone walls,
a wooden roof,
no monument
to duke or state—
if God drops in
He'll know someone
was looking for Him.

American Poets Abroad: On Not Being British Poets

It may be piety
or vanity of voice
that rises in the chapel,
echoes in the fields
in the Adamic work
of naming beast & leaf,
celebrates the waking of the world.

It may be that our work here
is simply speaking to each other.
Hedgehog and lark
must move along without us.
A God who cannot hear us
cannot blame us.
A God who listens has always
right of refusal.

Viola

Given his casual attention to cartography,
she could have landed on the seacoast of Bohemia.
It was always hit or miss.

Was it the ebb and flow of tides
that smoothed the seaside stones
or mere imagination?

Had he seen the Adriatic here—
violet at the horizon, then emerald,
then clear as glass in the shallows—

he would never have supposed
that the fancy outworks nature.
She is already in love with Illyria.

She listens to the whisper of the water,
the murmur of the waves against the shore,
and hears a hundred promises.

Romance or a hungry bear
awaits her over the first green hill.
So far, she likes her chances.

Monkey Music

Weary Willie
For Emmett Kelly

Sweeping up
after the big cats,
the tumblers, the jugglers,
the white-faced clowns,
he turns at last to the spotlight.
Not like a sequined acrobat,
but with the patience of a skivvy
he pokes his broom at the taunting spot
trying to gather a little heap
of happy days.

Everything Happens to Me
Chet Baker 1959

Heroin has not yet taken everything:
his face, as stunning as a starlet's,
his teeth, his embouchure, his life.

And he is singing a silly song
about rained-out golf dates,
noisy parties and complaining neighbors,
measles and mumps, all
maudlin metaphors for lost love,

As if it were the saddest song in the world.

New Yorker Cartoon Dog

He is an ordinary dog—
no Westminster Show poseur
or cocktail party wag.
He summons our nostalgia for that reader
where we learned to see Spot run.

But now he's found that there is neither
wit nor warmth in human utterance.
"Bad dog" passes all too often for bon mot,
"Good dog" a paltry substitute
for a companionable chat.

When he is off the leash—
checking on e-mail at the office
or having a drink at the corner bar
with a couple of friends—
the dumb show ends.

He has a way of pointing out the obvious,
we tend to listen,
he has an honest face.

Bouquet of Daffodils For Daffy Duck

A little difficulty with the S
is just a small impediment
to your unlikely eloquence,
but someone else is always holding the pen,
drawing up obstacles, sketching a fall.

I have learned to celebrate
your triumphs and your smiles,
rare as duck's teeth in a world
of stutter-stepping in the dark,
dodging anvils, shotguns, dynamite.

We all go a little daffy sometimes.
The merry-go-round breaks down for us all.

Shark Week

One boffo blockbuster and then
his story falls apart. The plot

unfolds, an origami menace
ill-conceived. His talent lies

in circling below, no talk show
gabfest for this mouthpiece. Advocates

and lenders fasten on his salty
coat tails, looking for that edge.

It's no surprise his sequels flop,
but he keeps on the move.

Not much remains of him to speak of
when the circling stops.

His bones are coral made,
his teeth are souvenirs.

Spaghetti Western Hero

His costume will be almost colorless—
no mayday red bandana
though he leans a little to the left
in the economy of death.

Filling the coffins at a craftsman's pace,
keeping the carpenter busy but not rushed,
tucking the rules of genre under his hat,
finding the noose is just another loophole,

he works in the dust at his solemn trade
backed by a music of preposterous joy.

Tuba Player

He won't be heard
lofting those haunting notes
over the fire escape
into the August night.

He won't be found
blowing cool fire
after hours
when the squares have left the club.

Wrapped up in it,
he wagers
his lumbering silhouette
against the skyward thrust of the trumpet.
Salvation is small comfort.

Backlot

You know what will happen
when you look in her eyes.
You've been to the movies,
missed out on the easy roles:
somebody else is walking up
to the drunken cowboys
shooting up the town,
the motorcycle gang,
the werewolf looking
for a place to settle down.
Somebody else is saying
"This is a quiet town.
We don't want trouble."

Dodge

What you want to leave behind
follows you everywhere.

When the dealer is run out of town,
the next is a stage away.

It's not his fault
you draw to an inside straight.

The fellow who plays piano
for Belle and her girls

wishes he'd stayed in Saint Louis.
You wouldn't argue the point.

Your only hope is that the script is lost,
that the school marm takes the bullet

and the dance hall girl is saved,
those dark eyes forever yours.

The Count to His Lover

Mother warned me about girls like you
who would bare white throats at midnight
and recant in the light of day.

Throw away the garlic choker
you are wearing now like a perfect prude.
As though it wasn't always you.

As though a man of my persuasion
could resist your overbite.
Didn't I ask you nicely?

Enter my house and come of your own free will.
If I go skulking back to the churchyard now
like a fallen priest,

if I'm afraid to stay for breakfast because
something terrible might happen, never forget
in the end my heart has a stake in it too.

To the Queen

Your blossom is falling,
petals poison the air,
poison the comb, the apple.

You know that vanity and appetite
betray her. You've been there.
She is almost your apprentice.

Seven deadly sins surround her,
thinly disguised.
Grumpy is just dwarfed wrath.

Kisses cure nothing.
Only botched allegory
can save her now.

Hyde on Jekyll

Breasts like twin fawns, sings Solomon.
Jekyll reaches for his stethoscope
evading the panopticon of Spring
that finds me underneath his skin
that sees his hands clenched against my heart's arousal.

Scotland is no excuse for lack of candor.
Isn't an impenetrable dialect
cloak enough for what
despite a winter like cold steel against the flesh
arises green within us with the thaw?

The doctor hoards his antidotes
and dreams of lilies for the hearse.
I am awake. Make haste.
Desire is stronger than death.

Cold War

Berlin has everything we need.
Night is a tentative ally.
The fog turns streets
to labyrinths, and there's the wall
to climb or tunnel under,
always the fatal promise of the spotlight.

In the end it turns on our duplicity.
The German of the spy is never perfect.
His code is out of date.
The double agent hopes to turn again.
Love, such as it is,
offers less shelter than a hotel shade,
less warmth than lamplight.
Always we listen for footsteps,
await the other shoe.

In Defense of Catherine Deneuve

The women in France are getting older
by the minute, Jim.
The French have never been concerned.
Their souls serenely maculate
see the eternal woman
in the flesh. They've learned
that time—*jamais perdu*—
records her story
forgetting nothing that it always knew.
Catherine Deneuve may have to wait
for her defense.
Time hasn't finished
with her elegance.

Paperback Lady Private Eyes

find designer clothes at the thrift shop
like the look of the bad boys a little too much
have that elderly friend who can watch the dog
know a doc who can patch them up in a pinch

speak fluent menu French when occasion requires
go for a sidewalk hot dog most of the time
just quit smoking again and regret it
ruin their best pair of heels in the rain

learn how to cover a shiner with makeup
forget that they left the gun in the other purse
aren't above abusing a whiff of Chanel
wouldn't turn down a Scotch at a quarter to three

remember the precinct cop who owes them a favor
find out that the client with bucks is a crook
borrow a little black dress and look like a million
own you heart and soul till the end of the book.

Robert E. Wood teaches in the School of Literature, Media, and Communication at Georgia Tech. He attended The Polytechnic Institute of Brooklyn and earned a BS and MS in Mathematics. Subsequently he received a MA in English from Long Island University and a PhD in English from the University of Virginia.

Specializing in Renaissance Studies and Cinema, Wood has published film studies that include essays on Fosse, DePalma, and Verhoeven, as well as *The Rocky Horror Picture Show*. He is also the author of *Some Necessary Questions of the Play*, a study of *Hamlet* published by Bucknell University Press.

Wood's poetry has appeared in such journals as *Southern Humanities Review, South Carolina Review, Quiddity, Blue Fifth Review, North Dakota Quarterly, Poets and Artists,* and *Prairie Schooner.* Earlier chapbooks, *Gorizia Notebook* and *Sleight of Hand,* were published by Finishing Line Press. His book of ekphrastic poetry, *The Awkward Poses of Others*, published by WordTech, was awarded Author of the Year in Poetry by the Georgia Writers Association An anthology *On Occasion: Four Poets, One Year* (Poetry Atlanta Press) contains his work together with that of fellow writers Karen Head, Blake Leland, and JC Reilly.

Robert and his wife Carolyn live in Roswell, Georgia.

www.ingramcontent.com/pod-product-compliance
Lightning Source LLC
LaVergne TN
LVHW041559070426
835507LV00011B/1190